All Aboard

Freight Trains

by Jenna Lee Gleisner

Bullfrog
Books

Ideas for Parents and Teachers

Bullfrog Books let children practice reading informational text at the earliest reading levels. Repetition, familiar words, and photo labels support early readers.

Before Reading

• Discuss the cover photo. What does it tell them?

• Look at the picture glossary together. Read and discuss the words.

Read the Book

• "Walk" through the book and look at the photos. Let the child ask questions. Point out the photo labels.

• Read the book to the child, or have him or her read independently.

After Reading

• Prompt the child to think more. Ask: Have you ever seen a freight train? Could you see what it was carrying?

Bullfrog Books are published by Jump!
5357 Penn Avenue South
Minneapolis, MN 55419
www.jumplibrary.com

Library of Congress Cataloging-in-Publication Data

Names: Gleisner, Jenna Lee, author.
Title: Freight trains / by Jenna Lee Gleisner.
Description: Bullfrog books edition.
Minneapolis, MN: Jump!, Inc., [2020]
Series: All aboard | Includes index.
Audience: Ages 5–8 | Audience: Grades K–1
Identifiers: LCCN 2019022732 (print)
LCCN 2019022733 (ebook)
ISBN 9781645272403 (hardcover)
ISBN 9781645272410 (ebook)
Subjects: LCSH: Railroad trains—Juvenile literature.
Classification: LCC TF580 .G54 2020 (print)
LCC TF580 (ebook) | DDC 385/.24—dc23
LC record available at https://lccn.loc.gov/2019022732
LC ebook record available at https://lccn.loc.gov/2019022733

Editors: Jenna Trnka and Sally Hartfiel
Designer: Molly Ballanger

Photo Credits: gk-6mt/iStock, cover; John Kirk/iStock, 1; ch123/Shutterstock, 3; BeyondImages/iStock, 4; Jurik Peter/Shutterstock, 5, 23tm; Bloomberg/Getty, 6–7, 23tl; i viewfinder/Shutterstock, 8–9, 23bm; Thomas Vieth/Dreamstime, 10–11; Dziobek/Shutterstock, 12; traveler1116/iStock, 12–13; s_oleg/Shutterstock, 14, 16–17; ghornephoto/iStock, 15; emrahkarakoc/iStock, 18, 23br; Bill Cobb/SuperStock, 19; Valentin Martynov/Shutterstock, 20–21; John Brueske/Shutterstock, 22; Nataly Studio/Shutterstock, 23tr; ifong/Shutterstock, 23bl; Ben Jeayes/Shutterstock, 24.

Printed in the United States of America at Corporate Graphics in North Mankato, Minnesota.

Table of Contents

Carrying Goods

Let's look at freight trains!

These trains carry goods.

They take them from one place to another.

Nice!

A conductor is in charge.
This person runs the train.

conductor

UPY
447

UNION
PACIFIC

7

A locomotive
is at the front.

It brings the power.

It pulls the cars.

locomotive

car

This train has
four locomotives.

They pull many cars!

These cars have open tops.

They are full.

They carry coal.

coal

These cars carry grain.

It is poured in from the top.
Then they are covered.

grain

tank car

Tank cars carry liquids.

Freight trains run on tracks.
They run across the country.

track

They run in cities, too.

Have you seen
a freight train?

Where was it?

Types of Freight Train Cars

There are many types of freight train cars.
Have you seen any of these?

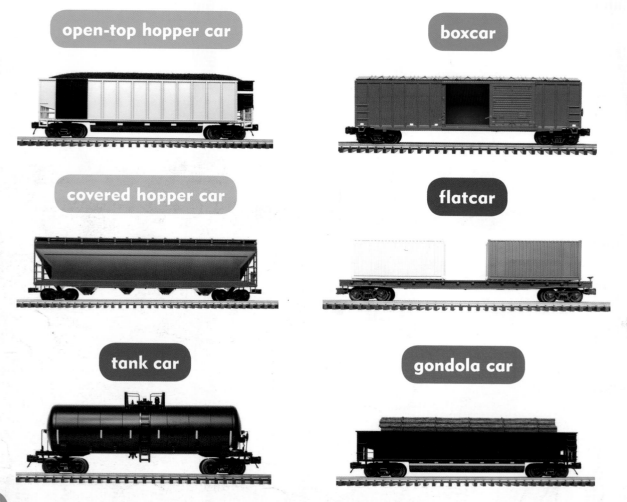

open-top hopper car

boxcar

covered hopper car

flatcar

tank car

gondola car

Picture Glossary

conductor
The person in charge of a train, its crew, and its freight.

freight
Goods, such as lumber, grain, or coal, that are carried.

grain
The seeds or fruit of food plants.

liquids
Substances that flow and can be poured.

locomotive
An engine used to push or pull railroad cars.

tracks
Rails or sets of rails for vehicles, such as trains, to run on.

Index

To Learn More

FACT SURFER

Finding more information is as easy as 1, 2, 3.

❶ Go to www.factsurfer.com

❷ Enter "freighttrains" into the search box.

❸ Choose your book to see a list of websites.